Buster Brown

and the

Cowboy

Richard Barker

*Studio portrait of
Buster Brown sitting
on a chair.*
© Brown Shoe
Company, Inc.
Courtesy:
Barbara Baker

*Dick Barker riding his horse. The saddle
is a Hartke and Sheets saddle, which is
on display at the Museum of Northwest
Colorado.*
Courtesy: Barbara Baker

©2011 Museum of Northwest Colorado
590 Yampa Ave.
Craig, CO 81625
970-824-6360
E-mail: musnwco@moffatcounty.net
Website: museumnwco.org

First edition
Printed in the United States of America

Library of Congress Control Number: 2010942899

ISBN: 978-0-9822935-8-4

Cover images:
Buster Brown in sailor uniform.
© Brown Shoe Company, Inc.
Courtesy: Barbara Baker

Postcard
© Brown Shoe Company, Inc.

Dick Barker on bronc.
Courtesy: Barbara Baker

Cover design by Mary Pat Dunn, Museum of Northwest Colorado, and Laurie Goralka Design
Book design by Laurie Goralka Design

Edited and published by the Museum of Northwest Colorado, Craig, Colorado, in association with:
Lifetime Chronicle Press
10614 Bostwick Park Rd.
Montrose, CO 81401
970-240-1153
chronicle@montrose.net

Dedication

This book is dedicated to Barbara Barker Terrill Baker who so generously donated her father's manuscript to the Museum to use for this publication. Not only did her father's writings tell the story of a little boy who so desperately wanted to grow up to be a cowboy, but her own recollections of her growing-up years are delightful and charming.

Table of Contents

A Glimpse Into an Aggressive Advertising Campaign in the Early 1900s

At the beginning of the last century, a cartoonist by the name of R. F. Outcault created the character Buster Brown and his dog, Tige, for the Sunday comic strips. The two quickly became so popular that Outcault was beset with requests to use them as advertising resources. With a vigour that would be appreciated in today's highly competitive markets, Buster Brown soon became a common household name.

The original drawing of Buster Brown.
Courtesy: Museum of Northwest Colorado

Depending on his mood, Mr. Outcault would sell the rights to use the Buster Brown name for anywhere from several dollars to a couple hundred dollars. Because of the liberal sale of these rights, the much-admired little boy was soon found endorsing a wide variety of products and novelties.

But the Brown Shoe Company, Inc., by far, capitalized the most on this trendy young man, as it branched out from shoes into articles of clothing. Even today, the Brown Shoe Company, Inc. is still in the business of manufacturing shoes.

Mary Pat Dunn

Introduction

Richard "Dick" Barker

I n 1906, the Brown Shoe Company began searching for a
young boy look-alike to use in advertising shows. Richard
Barker, aged seven, was chosen, much to his despair and his
mother's gratification. He spent the ensuing six years traveling
throughout the country dressed in red velvet and sporting long
golden tresses. The only bright spot, from his perspective in
these dismal circumstances, was the wonderful companionship
of his dog, Tige.

During this time, his heart longed passionately for the
Wyoming country he had first glimpsed on a tour west in the winter of 1907. Dick wanted to be a cowboy.

In 1913, he made his last appearance as the famous little
character and received a long-awaited visit to the barbershop. He
entered Western Military Academy, attending until he enlisted in
the army at the onset of World War I. Upon his discharge in 1919,
he returned to the Academy and graduated in 1920.

In 1923, accompanied by his young bride, Virginia, the reluc-
tant dandy finally "came home" as he made his way over the Rocky
Mountains and into the Yampa Valley. The following years held
many challenges for the couple. Ranch life and rodeoing are not
the most lucrative of enterprises in any time. Whenever finances
were stretched to the limit, Richard would reenter active military
service to bolster the family fortunes. In his later years, he led
covered wagon tours on the old Overland Trail.

His daughter, Barbara, commented that it was only his work
as the Buster Brown character and his stints in the service (both
of which he loathed) that ever brought him any real financial

remuneration. The balance of his years were spent fulfilling his boyhood dream—living the variable existence of the Western cowboy while finding great comfort and pride in his wife and their daughter.

Mary Pat Dunn

Chapter 1

Richard Barker

M ost of the personal memoirs I've read start out, "I was born to poor but honest parents," and mine is no exception. At any rate, mine were poor enough to qualify. As to the honest part, I'll leave that for some future historian to decide.

My mother was born Beatrice Louise Sutton, the youngest of 14 children, in Newcastle, New Brunswick, Canada. Sometime during the 1880s, finding the grass greener on the other side of the fence, the Suttons moved to the United States, where my mother met and in 1898 married George Fletcher Barker, a native of West Boylston, Massachusetts.

Shortly after their wedding, my father joined the army and went off to the Spanish-American War where, according to Mother, he distinguished himself by playing the flute in the

Dick Barker's father, George Barker, left the family in 1903, leaving Dick and his mother, Beatrice, on their own.
Courtesy: Barbara Baker

regimental band. Mother also stated that he probably did more to demoralize the enemy by the sound of his playing than the whole regiment could have done with machine guns. Anyway he got safely home from the field of battle with nothing worse than a sore lip, from playing the flute.

According to Mother, my father was so clean and sanitary that he always donned white kid gloves before carving the turkey. Knowing Mother's propensity for exaggeration, I have entertained grave doubts as to the truth of this statement.

I was born December 6, 1899, in Framingham, Massachusetts, about as far away from Snake River, Wyoming, as one can get and still remain within the continental limits of the United States. I always suspected that my mother wished that I had been born a girl, as she tried hard enough to make me look like one.

Another cross that my mother had to bear was my father's love for horses. Any kind of horse, fast, slow, old or young. My mother couldn't care less if she ever saw a horse. Of course, I

took after my father and loved them, too. This fondness for the horse may have been the reason that my father, in the spring of 1903, hitched one to a buggy and drove off to parts unknown, not to be seen or heard from for eight long years.

*Dick Barker was born
December 6, 1899,
in Framingham,
Massachusetts, to George
and Beatrice Barker.*
Courtesy:
Barbara Baker

Chapter 2

Becoming the Buster Brown Character

A long about the turn of the century, a well-known cartoon-ist—Mr. R. F. Outcault—dreamed up a couple of characters he called "Buster Brown and his dog, Tige." They became popular Sunday comic strip personalities. So popular, in fact, that the Brown Shoe Company, Inc. of St. Louis, Missouri, a manufac-turer of children's shoes, purchased from Mr. Outcault the right to use the names for their product. It was further decided that if a boy and a dog resembling the two could be found, they'd be hired to tour the country, giving free entertain-ment to school kids, thereby glorifying the names of Buster Brown and Tige, and incidentally, promot-ing the sale of those particular shoes.

This studio portrait of Buster was taken in about 1907.
> © Brown Shoe Company, Inc.
> Courtesy:
> Barbara Baker

*Beatrice Sutton
Barker was born
in Newcastle, New
Brunswick, Canada,
and married George
Barker in 1898.*
Courtesy:
Barbara Baker

*In 1907, the manager
of Brown Shoe Co.,
Inc.saw Dick Barker
with his white-collared
outfit and golden curls
and likened him to
the cartoon character,
Buster Brown.*
© Brown Shoe Co., Inc.
Courtesy:
Barbara Baker

After my father left in 1903, Mother became, by necessity, the bread winner, and she tackled the job with gusto by starting a dancing school in Greenfield, Massachusetts. As you might guess, I was her first pupil, and since I was without any particular talent for either singing or dancing, it must have been a discouraging proposition for her. Mother was a fighter, though, and even if she was only five feet tall and weighed in at a good healthy 90 pounds, nothing looked too big for her. I have always contended that she would fight a crocodile in eight feet of water and give him the first two bites. Consequently, I learned to sing and dance, after a fashion.

Buster and his mother traveled throughout the United States and Mexico, advertising Buster Brown Shoes for the Brown Shoe Company, Inc.

© Brown Shoe Co., Inc.
Courtesy: Barbara Baker

In the spring of 1907 when I was seven years old and complete with golden curls, a lace collar and an expression on my face of utter disillusionment with the world in general and dancing schools in particular, there arrived in Greenfield the general manager of the Brown Shoe Company, Inc. Through some trick of fate, he heard about me and that I looked like the Buster Brown character of the comic strip. He came to see and remained to watch me perform, as Mother, with the aid of a sharp stick and a kitchen chair, put me through my paces.

Well, as they say in books, the rest is history. He hired us to travel the United States advertising the Buster Brown Shoes for Boys and Girls. And so my future for the next seven years was sealed. At this news, I entertained mixed emotions. You see, I had already made up my mind to go west and be a cowboy.

The search for a prototype to play the Buster Brown character ended in my being selected. The matter of locating a "Tige" took longer. Where they finally found him I don't know, but find him they did, and for the next six years, we traveled together.

Chapter 3

Friends from the First

My first public appearance in the role of the Buster Brown character was in 1907 at the Jamestown Exposition near Norfolk, Virginia, and it was there that I met Tige. The Exposition was held to commemorate the founding of the first permanent English colony in America. I'm sure the arrival of Captain Christopher Newport and John Smith 300 years earlier couldn't have been viewed by the Indians with more apprehension than was felt by the welcoming committee the day Tige arrived. He was in a crate.

There must be a beautiful understanding between small boys and dogs. I could hardly get the crate open because his eager tongue kept getting in the way. If they had searched the world over they couldn't have come up with a better dog for the part of Tige, for he not only looked the part, but he had the personality it took to stand the vicissitudes of life that were to be his for the next six years.

It was apparent to all of us that here was a man of the world in looks, bearing and mental attitude. He was brindle, with a white patch on his broad chest; his jaw was square, not undershot, his legs were straight and muscular, and his compact little stern, topped by a medium-length tail carried defiantly erect, was a challenge to the world. He weighed in at a solid 40 pounds and regardless of what he ate, his weight never varied. And he ate anything—leftover shrimp from Antoine's in New Orleans to cold beans from the Parker House in Boston; it was all the same to Tige. I remember the time in Nuevo Laredo when, with tears streaming down his cheeks, he polished off a small helping of slightly used enchiladas.

Buster and Tige quickly became friends when they met at the Jamestown Exposition near Norfolk, Virginia, in 1907.
© Brown Shoe Company, Inc. Courtesy: Barbara Baker

He walked with a devil-may-care swagger, giving one the impression that he wore a disreputable felt hat cocked over his eyes and had a toothpick in his mouth. His scars of battle were of the romantic type, like the one he got in San Francisco from a dignified collie during a passage of arms over a lady cocker. It started coyly under the left ear and ended at the corner of his mouth, so that ever afterwards he looked at the world with a sardonic grin. For all the skid-row appearance he acquired, I never knew a child who was afraid to walk up to him, nor was he ever known to harm one.

Chapter 4

Adventures High and Low

His exploits were many and varied, and life with Tige was never boring. Take the wheelchair incident at Atlantic City.

It was a warm Sunday afternoon and the boardwalk swarmed with people. Vacationers from nearby Philadelphia were out in force enjoying the sun, sand and surf. Many were walking, but others rode in a type of wheelchair that could be hired by the hour, day or week, with or without an attendant to do the pushing. In the event no hired pusher was desired, a member of the family, usually the long-suffering husband, did the honors while the wife rode in effortless ease. It was a combination like this that caused all the trouble.

Mother and I were working our way through the crowd. I led Tige by a chain leash—he ate the leather ones. Mother was worried.

"I wish you had left him at the hotel," she said. "If there's a dog anywhere, he'll find it."

We continued on, slowly threading our way between people and wheelchairs. Mother was still worried, and when she worried, she talked.

"I don't think they allow loose dogs on the boardwalk, but you never know. Are you sure you're holding that chain tightly?"

"Oh, yes. Don't worry, Mother, he can't get away from me. I've got him!"

"You've said that before! I can't enjoy myself while I'm always thinking what may happen when we have that dog out." Mother paused to peer around for strange dogs. "Are you sure you have a good tight grip on that chain?"

Tige not only looked the part of the cartoon character but had his personality, also.
© Brown Shoe Company, Inc.
Courtesy: Barbara Baker

"Yes, Mother, don't worry." I looked down on the sand where the breakers were rolling. "Mother, can I go swimming?"

"No, you may not go swimming. You just hold that dog."

It was then we met the wheelchair, head on. It was pushed by a small, timid-looking man and was occupied by a very large, overdressed and bejeweled lady. The press of people surrounding us made maneuvering difficult. We were forced to wait, face-to-face, until a thinning in the crowd would allow us to pass.

So help me, I didn't see the tiny dog the woman was nestling to her vast bosom, its lolling tongue looking like a red lavalier. Tige saw it, though. You can bet your sweet life he saw it! He jerked the chain from my careless hand and was off in a scrambling rush. If they gave medals for saving dogs, I'd be the most decorated American since Sergeant York.

Reviving Tige was never difficult, but the strategic withdrawal from the field of carnage after these little engagements took a cool head and a gift for diplomacy. Mother was never any help, because at the first clash of fang on fang, she would be off and away to meet us later— usually a lot later.

I had gotten Tige a short distance in the clear when that meek little man—egged on by his wife, no doubt—caught us. I was brought to a halt by a firm grip on my neck. (I remember he suddenly impressed me as being considerably larger.)

"Is that cur yours?" His voice was loud and threatening. "What's your name? Whose boy are you?" He shook me.

"Yes, sir," I quavered, "he's mine."

Still holding me, he glanced back to the crowd surrounding his wife. I thought he was looking for a cop and prepared for the worst. He released me instead and, bending down, whispered, "Run, kid, get out of here," and then he added in the voice of a man who has at long last broken the yoke of oppression, "I wish to God he'd killed it!"

We took his advice and ran.

Chapter 5

On the Road Together

I t was our job to advertise our employer's merchandise, and to do so we went anywhere shoes were worn—and some places where they weren't. In those long-gone days before radio and television, this was the best means of reaching the prospective buyers. We gave our show anywhere, sometimes in hired theaters or halls, but often in the open air on knocked-together platforms. Our props were simple—a piano, a stool for Tige to sit on and a table for the display of samples were all that were needed to launch our campaign.

It's been nearly 60 years, but I blush when I think what we served up as entertainment. It was all free but even so, the audiences still got cheated. Mother made the opening address. The warm-up, so to speak. Among other things, she'd make a stirring plea for silence on the grounds that "Buster is just a little boy." A plea, I might add, that usually went unheeded into the unwashed ears of young America.

After some semblance of order was established, she'd strike a few chords on the piano and Tige and I would dash out, all gaiety and laughter—me to sing our opening song and Tige to his stool, which he sometimes leaped at with such gusto that he'd slide off on the opposite side and land on his fat rear. This always brought screams of delight from the audience.

Since my voice was anything but robust, I couldn't sing much louder than a mouse could squeak. This was probably a fortunate thing, because I couldn't carry a tune anyway.

Our contract stipulated that I wear the Buster Brown costume at all times. It was fire-engine red; the hat was what is called a "tam," and it, too, was red. It was secured to the back of my head by an elastic band that went under the chin. I wore a black leather belt that sagged under my stomach like a tired hammock, and my starched white collar, tied with a black Windsor, made a trampoline for my golden curls to bounce on. I didn't just exactly make friends on sight, and I was forever in a fight or a footrace. When you come right down to it, Tige was the only friend I had, but he was a good one.

Buster was promoting the Brown Shoe Co., Inc. at Grove City, Pennsylvania.

© Brown Shoe Company, Inc.
Courtesy: Museum of Northwest Colorado

Chapter 6

Always a Gentleman

—————————

T ige had a remarkable sense of direction and an uncanny
ability to find me. Once, he got loose in the basement of a
strange hotel, one we had never before visited. Our room
was on one of the higher floors, but when we opened our door in
the morning, there he was, waiting.

In Pittsburgh, he was stolen. We had the entire police force
on the lookout for him, but he found his way back to the old Hotel
Henry without help. He was dragging two feet of rope and had
a badly mangled ear to prove that his enforced absence had not
been without incident.

It was in Chicago he ran afoul of the law. While enjoying an
unexpected moment of freedom, he wandered out of the Brevoort
Hotel and followed a lady dog of loose morals to a far part of
the city. Finding himself a long way from home, his ardor cooled
and, being understandably tired after a night of wine, women and
song, he saw no reason to exert himself further by a long walk
home when carriages had always taken him to his hotel before.

With the pleasing prospect of a comfortable ride in the warm
spring sunshine, he simply hunted up a hack and got in—taxis
were unknown in those days. Poor Tige! How was he to know
the difference between a public conveyance and a private one?
It stood by the curb in front of an impressive house on Michigan
Avenue, the door invitingly open.

We hadn't realized he was gone until the police phoned us.
The coachman, unable to induce Tige to get out, had driven to a
police station where they got our name from his collar. They told
us that the coachman would bring Tige to the Brevoort. I saw the

arrival and I must say it was a dramatic spectacle.

First came the satiny black horses, the silver trimmings on the harness reflecting the rays of the morning sun; the dignified driver in spotless livery guiding the elegant coach, its wheels like four spinning bouquets. It drew up at the entrance and the doorman, not knowing who might be arriving, but taking no chances, opened the door and, stepping back, gravely bowed. Out came Tige like the scion of some prominent family, home after a night on the town, dirty, dusty, bleary eyed and just a bit pleased with himself.

© Brown Shoe Company, Inc.
Courtesy: Barbara Baker

Chapter 7

Father Comes and Goes

T he next time that I saw my father was accidental, and the incident was very unusual. It happened after my mother and I had been traveling over the country as the Buster Brown character for three years. We had just gotten off the train late one night at Fresno, California, and gone to a hotel. My mother registered for a room and the clerk called a porter to take our

George Barker is on the right. The other man is unknown.
Courtesy: Barbara Baker

baggage up. When we got to the room, I offered the porter a quarter, which he refused to accept.

I was only 11 years old at the time, but I can still remember how uncomfortable he looked and how he stared at me. He was my father, but because of some feminine quirk of Mothers, I was not to know it until nine years later when she got a letter from someone in Del Rio, Texas, relating that he was there, was a very sick man and needed help. I went to Del Rio at once, but too late, as he had recovered and left with no forwarding address. I tried repeatedly to trace him without success, and I must conclude that somewhere he fills an unmarked grave. I have a snapshot of us riding a couple of horses near Fresno, for he traveled with Mother and me around California for about a month. On Mother's orders, I called him "Pal" during that month. He was a nice guy and I liked him. One of the horseback rides we took was on two livery stable horses from Los Angeles to Hollywood. The purpose of the trip was to inspect the home of the newest craze—moving pictures—and I was fortunate enough to meet Fatty Arbuckle and other stars of the silent screen.

Chapter 8
A Day at the Races

W̶e gave our shows where the crowds were thickest and state and county fairs were favorite spots. One I remember particularly was in Kansas and, like any other country fair, it had the usual attractions: a merry-go-round, ferris wheel and side shows where, for a small charge, you could watch exotic dancers gyrate and, of course, they had games of skill where, for

© Brown Shoe Company, Inc.
Courtesy: Barbara Baker

© Brown Shoe Company, Inc.
Courtesy: Barbara Baker

a quarter, you might win a valuable prize, though no one ever did. In addition, this fair was having a race meet.

They had a little old half-mile track, rough, dusty and run down. A sun-bleached grandstand leaned drunkenly and groaned alarmingly as the rabid race fans filled its splintery seats. Directly across the track from this they had made a stage by laying planks between two dry goods boxes. It was from this lofty platform that Tige and I were to advertise the virtue of the Buster Brown Shoes—between races, naturally.

Tige's post during the performance was on a piano stool and, as he grew older, he sometimes went to sleep and fell off. This was always good for a big laugh. We were about half through the show and Tige was blissfully sleeping when out on the track wandered a nondescript hound dog. Some trouble developed directly under his tail—a restless flea perhaps—so he was forced to sit down and propel himself by front drivers alone until the itch was relieved.

A wave of laughter from the interested spectators drew his attention to the grandstand and he regarded this phenomena with sad, puzzled eyes, his head tilting alternately from right to left. It was at this moment the forgotten flea chose to renew the attack.

With a yelp of indignant agony, the hound whirled like a dervish in an attempt to make contact with his rear and, failing, he fell, thus effectively stopping the caboose and allowing the front end to reach the place that hurt. He made quite a satisfactory assault there, accompanied by more laughter from the stands.

It was at this moment good old Tige elected to awake. He opened his eyes, yawned mightily, noted how far along the show had progressed, and was about to return to dreamland when his glance was arrested by the lone hound below. The next instant he was flying through the air like a kamikaze pilot, and as those pilots sometimes did, he missed the target, landing with a mighty grunt and an upflinging of debris directly behind the unsuspecting dog.

The startled hound gave a bellow of mortal terror and left with the celerity and singleness of purpose of a quarter horse coming out of a starting gate. The race began fairly even and progressed that way to the first turn, at which point the hound, having a length lead, looked back to see how he was doing. Immediately, his lead widened.

On the back stretch, Tige was gamely holding his own, but he wasn't built for distance. If it hadn't been for treacherous footing at the clubhouse turn, due to a muddy spot left from last night's shower, the race would have ended just that way. But it's from such mishaps that hope springs. Tige, his bursting eyes seeing the flying quarry close at hand, put on a surge of speed and the gap rapidly closed, but not quite.

The snap of Tige's jaws brought from the hound a scream, together with a spectacular leap of some 10 feet. This put him in the lead to stay, and he made it under the wire, disappearing through a forest of legs, his progress to safety marked by hysterical howls dying in the distance. Tige staggered in a bad last, his eyes popping out like two avocados.

So ended a day at the races. Tige stole the show. I couldn't quite get the attention of that audience again.

Chapter 9

The End of the Road

It was becoming more and more apparent that our traveling days must soon end. I was getting too big for the part, and my neglected schooling was beginning to cause comment. By the time 1913 rolled around, I was getting too big to be going around with curls. People, especially young people about my age, were making so much fun of me that life was just about unbearable. No doubt today I would be right in style, but I shudder to think what would have happened to one of today's hippies had he showed up without a bodyguard in 1913.

Our last show was given at Yuma, Arizona, and from there, Tige and I made our last long train trip together home to Massachusetts, where Tige spent his remaining days. Ten minutes after arriving, I got a hair cut—a short one.

Tige mellowed a lot in his later years, due, I think, to a combination of advanced age and good company. He made friends instead of enemies of the neighborhood dogs, and because of his wide travels, he got to be a raconteur of note, a sort of fire-hydrant philosopher.

I have an old picture of him in front of me as I write; his honest eyes look straight into mine, even as they did over 50 years ago. I visited him on each of my vacations from school. We would talk over old times and have a lot of good laughs about our days on the road.

I always left him with reluctance, but for some reason, the last time I saw him was the worst. I think it must have been because he started to howl—he'd never howled before. Mother wrote me some time later that he'd died that night.

The last time Buster saw Tige was the hardest because he had to leave him. His mother told him later that Tige died that night.

© Brown Shoe
Company, Inc.
Courtesy:
Barbara Baker

Buster, on horseback, with two companions.

© Brown Shoe Company, Inc.
Courtesy: Barbara Baker

PERHAPS YOU DON'T PUNCH THE BAG, BUT IF YOU NEED STRENGTH, YOU HAVE BUT

TO EAT
BUSTER BROWN
BREAD

© Brown Shoe Company, Inc.
Courtesy: Museum of Northwest Colorado

© Brown Shoe Company, Inc.
Courtesy: Museum of Northwest
Colorado

© Brown Shoe Company, Inc.
Courtesy: Museum of Northwest
Colorado

TIGE: "YOU GET GOOD GOODS AT FLETCHER AND BISSETT'S,

October-1910
Sun. Mon Tue Wed. Thur. Fri. Sat.
                            1
2   3   4   5   6   7   8
9 10 11 12 13 14 15
16 17 18 19 20 21 22
23 24 25 26 27 28 29
30 31

RESOLVED
THAT YOU CAN'T GET
BLOOD OUT OF TURNIP.
BUT YOU CAN GET CIDER.
OUT OF AN APPLE. YOU
MUST GO TO A GOOD STORE
TO GET GOOD GOODS.
BUSTER BROWN.

Buster and Beatrice.
© Brown Shoe
Company, Inc.
Courtesy:
Barbara Baker

*Buster and an
unidentified
young
girl were
photographed
in a studio set
in Petoskey,
Michigan,
1910.*
© Brown Shoe
Company, Inc.
Courtesy:
Barbara Baker

Buster in wagon, circa 1908.
© Brown Shoe Company, Inc. Courtesy: Barbara Baker

Buster riding a horse.
© Brown Shoe Company, Inc. Courtesy: Barbara Baker

Chapter 10

Becoming a Man

I first saw Wyoming during the winter of 1907 and for me, it was love at first sight. I still remember with pleasure the cold windy day we got off the Union Pacific train at Medicine Bow and today, when I smell the smoke from wood and coal fires, that day returns to me and is one of my fondest memories.

Some weeks later, we found ourselves in the town of Sheridan with the prospect of a trip to Buffalo giving us pause for thought. In 1907, Buffalo was an inland town—that is, the railroad had not yet reached it, consequently when one desired to make that trip, one went by horse-drawn conveyance. To

Buffalo, Wyoming

Courtesy: Barbara Baker

make it more interesting, on the day we left Sheridan, it was 40 degrees below zero and there was a howling Wyoming blizzard blowing. It was 40 miles to Buffalo, and it was the longest 40 miles and the lowest 40 degrees I had ever experienced up to that time. We traveled in a two-seated carriage pulled by two horses, and we made the trip in two hitches, staying one night at a ranch near the present location of Story, Wyoming.

I don't remember how many trips we made to Wyoming during those years, but I'm sure of at least five, and each time I liked it better than the last. I liked the mountains, the deserts and the people, and I made up my mind that someday I'd live there. I spent each vacation from school somewhere in Wyoming, except one when I worked for a steer outfit near Cottulla, Texas, and one year in the oil fields near Healdton, Oklahoma.

Obviously, when we finished with the Brown Shoe Company, Inc. in 1913, I had had no schooling; traveling constantly forbid that. I could read—Mother helped me there—but anything to do with other school subjects, with the exception of the geography

Dick attended Governor Dummer Academy in South Byfield, Massssachusetts, in 1914.

Courtesy: Barbara Baker

of the United States, was a mystery to me. In order to catch up with my contemporaries, I had a year at the Governor Dummer Academy at South Byfield, Massachusetts. The following year, 1915, I went to Western Military Academy at Alton, Illinois.

𝔇ummer 𝔄cademy

THE school receives both boarding and day scholars from the age of ten years and the fifth grade, and by a systematic course of study extending over eight years, prepares them thoroughly for college or business life. While doing this, the school aims to discover the possibilities of each student and to train him so that in utilizing his possibilities, he may think clearly and soundly, and, with widened perceptions and strengthened affections, seek eagerly his proper place in the community, render full service, and advance high purposes.

The daily life and interests of the boys are carefully considered by the masters. The fact is appreciated that they are personally responsible for the students during the entire twenty-four hours of the day. The masters also realize that the training in morals, manners and habits, which is the natural responsibility of the parent, is for a time delegated to them.

The size of the school enables the masters to know each boy well. The social life is varied and interesting, but the distractions of city life are eliminated. The school is the center of interest.

Courtesy: Barbara Baker

D.B.

Religious Life WHILE the school is a Congregational foundation, it is in fact non-sectarian. It insists on some positive religion as of great importance to the developing boy and seeks to enrich his life by teaching the love of truth and the significance of worship and aspiration.

The exercises of each day begin with morning prayer. On Sunday, attendance at the morning service of the Byfield Parish (Congregational) Church, or of some other church selected by parent or guardian, is required.

Courtesy: Barbara Baker

THE cost of tuition and board is $600.00 a year. Day pupils pay $150.00 **Expenses** a year tuition. Students residing in Byfield Parish pay $50.00 a year tuition. (See also Scholarships.)

Books, stationery, and laundry are furnished at list rates.

Day pupils may take luncheon at the Commons at $1.50 per week.

A laboratory fee of $5.00 is charged those taking courses in chemistry or physics.

The graduation fee is $5.00.

An annual subscription of $10.00 for athletics is asked from each student.

A deposit of $15.00 is required of each boarding student at time of registration.

Bills for tuition are invariably due as follows: one half at the beginning of the first term, one half at the opening of second term (January). No abatement of tuition for absence for any cause will be made except in cases of sickness lasting a term, when the loss is shared equally by the school and the parents.

R 3 3

In 1915, Dick attended Western Military Academy in Alton, Illinois, and again in 1919, graduating with the class of 1920.
Courtesy:
Barbara Baker

Courtesy:
Barbara
Baker

With our participation in World War I in 1917, I enlisted in the army. I came out of that with a commission as Second Lieutenant of Infantry. My rapid promotion was due entirely to my military school training and not for any excellence on my part.

When I was discharged from the army on January 19, 1919, I went back to Western Military Academy and stayed to graduate with the class of 1920.

After graduating, I just drifted. I tried first to get back to Wyoming by catching a freight out of St. Louis, but I only got as far as St. Joseph, where the law picked me up for vagrancy. Since I was underage, they got in touch with Mother, who sent the money to get me back to St. Louis. After three nights in the St. Joseph jail, it didn't take much coaxing for me to produce Mother's address. At this point, I carefully reviewed my past life and decided it might be better if I got a job and earned enough money to get me back to Wyoming. The memory of that St. Joe holding pasture may have had something to do with my decision.

Jobs in 1923 were not too plentiful, at least not for one whose only recommendation in the way of past employment was seven years as a child freak, a few months in the army, and three days spearing butts in the St. Joseph jail. After a lot of refusals, I finally landed a job selling ribbons and other intimate items at Famous-Barr and Co., a big department store in St. Louis. I went to work at 1:00 p.m. on a fine spring afternoon and by 2:30, I decided I was not cut out for that line of work, so I picked up my hat and walked out. They still owe me for an hour-and-a half labor.

It was a lucky thing I walked out on that job just at the time I did, though I'll admit I was at a loss to know what I was going to do next, when one of those coincidences you least expect met me before I'd gone a block from Famous-Barr & Co., in the shape of one of my best friends and schoolmates from Western Military Academy. His name was Bud Douglas and he lived in a small town about 30 miles east of St. Louis. Hillsboro, Illinois, was the name of the place, and outside of being a farming community, its main excuse for existence was the Eagle-Pitcher Zinc Smelter, a large concern that not only hired a lot of men, but supported a darned good semipro baseball team.

After the usual handshaking and backslapping, I told Bud I was having a lot of trouble finding congenial employment by the merchant princes of St. Louis. It was then Bud suggested I come with him to Hillsboro and strike the Eagle-Pitcher up for a job. He said the baseball team was sadly in need of a second baseman and while I would have to work on the furnaces shoveling blue powder into retorts, the hours were fine, only about three and a half hours a day, from 4:00 a.m. to 7:30 a.m. The pay was good and I could play baseball the rest of the time. Since I had played the infield three years for the first team at Western Military Academy, he was sure I would get the job.

So I worked and played baseball all summer. We won 16 games and only lost one. Wyoming, here I come!

Dick played baseball for the Eagle-Pitcher Zinc Smelter baseball team in Hillsboro, Illinois.
                    Courtesy:
            Barbara Baker

Chapter 11

A Change of Plans

The best laid plans don't always work out. Oh, I got to Wyoming alright, but I made a detour through Oklahoma, where I worked in the oil fields out of Ardmore, Wynnewood and Healdton until the following spring, when I contracted a sickness common to most oil field roughnecks and had to quit. Back in St. Louie, I spent most of the summer getting well and renewing old acquaintances from my days at Western Military Academy. I had quite a summer carousing around, going on moonlight boat trips down the Mississippi and generally leading the carefree life of rakehelly young bachelors. It was on one of those moonlight boat trips that I met Virginia.

Late one afternoon, Gene Diesing, a friend of mine from school days, called me and said a bunch of high school kids were going on the *SS St. Paul* for a three-hour trip down the river. Of course, I went. Gene and I made a tour around the boat, looking over the offering of girls with the critical eyes of a couple of horse traders at the Keenland sales judging the latest crop of fillies. A couple danced close by me and the girl looked cuter than a button. She had short blonde hair, was about 15 hands high (five feet) and she wore a short black-and-white checkered gingham dress.

She refused to dance with me the first time I asked her, which made her look better than ever. The second time I asked her, she said, "Yes." I danced with her the rest of the evening and never again turned her loose. We were married a short time later. I still consider that the luckiest night of my life.

Dick and Gin February 2, 1922, on their wedding day.
Courtesy: Barbara Baker

Whoever it was who said two can live as cheaply as one should reserve a room for himself at the nearest funny farm. That first few months we were married, we both lost weight. I worked for a while in a filling station. One night, a very convincing looking man with a six shooter that had the biggest hole in the barrel I've ever gazed into came into the station and asked me for all the money in the joint. He was very courteous as he asked me for the money and I, not to be outdone in courtesy, gave it to him. I don't like to exaggerate, but I never passed the West Portal of the Moffat Tunnel in later years without thinking about that gun.

Next I tried being an auto mechanic, but on my third day, the outfit went bankrupt, so all I got out of that deal was a 1914 Model T Ford with a brass radiator. I sold it for $10.00, but not before Virginia and I had some interesting rides. It kept us entertained, watching things fall off like the hood and a wheel, and once we lost the gas tank, which was bigger than the car. It held 40 gallons and was mounted behind the bucket seats. That was O.K., though, because I don't think it ever had more than two gallons in it at a time. We replaced it with a lard bucket.

Haig Searcy's father was the head of the horse and mule department across the river at the East St. Louis Stockyards. I had gone to school with Haig and he got me a job there which, while it didn't pay much, was certainly more to my liking than any of my previous jobs. I didn't mind in the least the cleaning of the mule barns, an endless task, because I got to do a lot of riding, too. There was always someone who wanted a horse ridden before, during or after the sales. I caught them coming and going, and at $5.00 a ride, I did O.K.

Joker, one of Dick's favorite horses, in St. Louis, 1922.

Courtesy: Barbara Baker

Across from the big main gate going into the stockyards and behind the local speakeasy, there ran a big craps game day and night, so in addition to my other income, I got another $5.00 for working a short shift as a shill. Virginia was not too happy about this means of providing the daily groceries, but she was a darn sight unhappier the night the law raided the joint and we all got stuffed in the pokey. The man who banked the game came the next morning and bailed us out.

So far I hadn't made any great success of life. That is to say, I sure hadn't made any discernible breach in the walls of financial security, but hope springs eternal for the human spirit, and I still had hopes.

I'm sure I would have gotten back to Wyoming eventually anyway, but I might never have seen or heard of Snake River if it hadn't been for Herman Luyties. He wandered into the mule barn one day while I was shoveling manure and introduced himself. He said he was there on a visit and had heard of me through mutual friends and wanted to meet me. He had a homestead in Routt County near the Wyoming line. It was situated a couple of miles south of the Temple Ranch at a place we know as Spine Kope.

Chapter 12

Reaching Snake River

After days of talking, Herman and I agreed to throw in together. He had a small place near Morrison, just outside of Denver, where he had a couple of horses, one old pinto and a three-year-old unbroke sorrel filly. The deal was that Virginia and I were to come to Denver, pick up the two horses and bring them by truck to Steamboat Springs, and then ride them over to Snake River from there.

The Stinking Water ranch home on Snake River, Wyoming.
Courtesy: Barbara Baker

And that's the way we got to Snake River. We stayed one night with Millbank Frands at Clark and on a fine spring day in the year 1923, we came over the hill above Three Forks and got our first look at the valley that was to be our home from then on, although I don't think either one of us knew it at the time. It's always been a satisfaction to me that the first look at our future home was from the back of a horse.

We spent that first night in Luyties' cabin at Spine Kope. The cabin—half log, half lumber—stood in a grove of aspen trees. It was, and still is, a beautiful spot. The cabin is gone now, but the trees are still there, and in spite of the addition of some sheep corrals, it remains a most picturesque location. We used to hold the Fourth of July picnic there and ranchers from up and down the river came to celebrate. The entertainment aside from the food, which was excellent, consisted of horse racing, bronc riding and the consumption of much Kemmerer whiskey, the last a delicacy noted for its strength, if not its bouquet.

I still remember how Clarence Decker, after a thin touch of this fine imported nectar, made the greatest bareback ride on a Salisbury horse I have ever seen. The fact that there were no fences at that time, and that after the bronc quit bucking, it lit out at a dead run only added to the show. Wes Fleming and I,

The barn sat next to the house, with a garden between them.
Courtesy: Barbara Baker

who were supposed to pick Clarence up, found ourselves somewhat outclassed. I remember we got him headed about halfway
to Temples'. As for the horse, he was picked up in the fall on
Battle Creek above the Smiley place.

Chapter 13

Learning the Frontier Life

M y partnership with Herman Luyties did not prove to be the most remunerative deal I ever made and soon came to a screaming halt. If it hadn't been for Mr. and Mrs. Harry Temple, Sr., I don't know whether Virginia and I would have made it on Snake River or not. As it was, Mr. Temple gave me a job feeding cattle all winter while Mrs. Temple, whose generous heart and great hospitality was a byword in the country, took 17-year-old

Dick punching cows at the Focus Ranch, owned by the Temples.
Courtesy: Barbara Baker

Virginia under her wing and showed her the difference between cooking a meal and just opening a can.

It has always been a wonder to me how Virginia adapted to the ways of the country the way she did. Here she was, a city girl—an accomplished musician who had never been further west than Grand Avenue in St.Louis but who fit in out here as if she'd been born here and who faced with courage, if not with delight, the problem of a dirt roof (our first), that in rainy weather not only leaked muddy water, but muddy water complete with worms that had a diabolical knack of falling into the frying pan while she was frying the bacon. I salute her and join her in thanking the good Lord that those days are gone forever.

The following spring, while Virginia remained under the kind care of Mrs. Temple, I threw in with an outfit to run wild horses down in the lower country. It was made up of some darned good men: Wes Fleming, Shorty Creel, Guy McNurlin, Earnest Lang and Ed Niel. Ed was the cook. I was along to learn and I had some mighty good teachers. The object of the expedition was to get rich. However, it didn't exactly work out that way. If it had only been a matter of trapping horses, we accomplished that alright, for we came up the river six weeks later with 200 head, some of them belonging to upper country people—for which we were supposed to get $5.00 a head for gathering (but never did)—and the rest unbranded. When we got to the old Pendland corral at Baggs, we split up the slicks between us.

Out of it all, I got a team of little bay mares that I had for 20 years and a sorrel stud that I had just as long and that my daughter rode to school for three years. It was bully good fun, though I wouldn't recommend it as a means of becoming financially secure in the foreseeable future. To me it was a fascinating life, and I did it each spring for three years!

Chapter 14

The First Homestead

A bout this time, I decided we'd better have something to call our own, so I gave $1,500 for the old Fisher place, consisting of 220 acres. There is nothing left of the old buildings but the barn, and it stands as a sentinel, defying the encroachment of changing times.

There is a sulfur spring on the place, a warm one with a good robust odor that caused my friends to name the ranch the "Stinking Water." It was a pretty good little home, though, especially when I homesteaded 640 acres that joined it on the south and ran from the road almost to the top of Three Forks Mountain.

This valuable piece of property was just good enough for a man to starve to death on. The only way it survived at all was for me to work out [off the ranch] to support it and for Virginia to give piano lessons to the offspring of Snake River. One of these pupils was Leonard Fleming of International Harvester fame. Leonard didn't quite make it to Carnegie Hall, but then neither did Pat and Mage Toole or Elmer Hartzel, who also were subjected to Virginia's teaching.

It was about this time that the last of the big cattle outfits had breathed their last, at least as far as this country was concerned, and we were all advised by the so-called experts to get down out of our saddles and get on milk stools—that the future of Snake River lay in how much cream we could ship. This did not exactly meet the approval of the high-heeled, horse-riding members of Snake River society, therefore most of them curled their tails over their backs and took off for Nevada. Among those who left on this exodus were Jack Alford, Heck Lytton and Clarence Crouse, just to name a few. Some waited a while, like Skinny Ayers, and when he left, he went to New Mexico, and Roge Rogerson left but came back later.

Chapter 15

Taking on the Dude Strings

I t looked like the riding days on Snake River were over, and they were for a number of years, so that if a man wanted to stay on horseback, he had to do the next best thing, which was break horses for the sheep outfits or wrangle dudes. I did both.

Jack Boyer, Sr., was a sheep man and a good one. He also had a dude ranch up the Savery and a lot of tip-top good horses, and he saved me from a milk stool by hiring me to take out pack trips and break horses. I worked for Jack off and on for five years, and he was one of the best bosses I ever had, and a darn fine gentleman, too.

Dick riding a bronc.

Courtesy: Barbara Baker

Jack Boyer riding a bronc on the Boyer Ranch, near Savery, Wyoming. Dick was the hazer for Jack Boyer.

Courtesy:
Barbara Baker

Dick on a bear hunting trip.
Courtesy: Barbara Baker

I remember the first pack trip I took out. Jack came out to the corral one morning just as I got in with the saddle horses.

"Dick, do you know where Hog Park is?"

"No," I said, "where is it?"

"Well, never mind, you can find it. Can you cook?"

"I've been known to—but not very good."

"That's alright," said Jack, "you're taking nine guests on a pack trip to Hog Park tomorrow."

I took those poor trusting dudes on the most extended, long-way around, nine day search for Hog Park they ever dreamed of in their wildest nightmares. Fortunately, it's a big park, so I finally found it, and the best of it was that they never suspected I was lost for the first eight days. I also had the same type of job with Ralph Salisbury on the Saddle Pocket Ranch, but by that time, I knew the high country well, so the dudes were somewhat safer.

During these years, I had joined the Officers Reserve Corps as a Second Lieutenant of Cavalry assigned for training to the old Seventh Cavalry, then stationed at Fort Bliss, Texas. This was Custer's old outfit, the one that lost the decision at the battle of the Little Big Horn in 1876. I think it was one of the last regiments

Taking guests on a pack trip, possibly in Hog Park.

Courtesy: Barbara Baker

Dick wrangled dudes and worked for sheep outfits to be able to stay on horseback.

Courtesy: Barbara Baker

to be mechanized in 1941, but when I went to Texas for training with them, it was strictly horses—no tanks allowed.

My reason for going into the Reserve Corps was not so much patriotic as economic. Each year, you got ordered for a nice two-week trip to Fort Bliss for training with troops and got paid for it, plus mileage. It made a pleasant change from ranch life, and both Virginia and I looked forward to going.

Chapter 16
A Joyous Addition

I remember the advent of 1929 for two very good reasons: one was the miserable spring weather, and the second and most important was that on March 4, while President-elect Hoover was making his inaugural speech, our daughter, Barbara, was born in Dixon. Dr. Noyes, of revered memory, was the attending physician at Nettie Terrill's—whose home was, at that time, considered to be Snake River's answer to Colorado General Hospital's maternity ward—was where the action took place.

Gin, pregnant with Barbara, at their Stinking Water ranch in Wyoming.
Courtesy: Barbara Baker

A very proud Dick Barker holding his daughter, Barbara, born in 1929.
Courtesy:
Barbara Baker

I was feeding cattle with Wes Fleming up at Gold Blossom when the word reached me via hand-cranked telephone and mounted messenger in the form of old John Gill, and I remember the celerity with which I saddled up Red Cloud and set sail for Dixon, reaching there just in time to be in on the grand finale.

Chapter 17

World War II Service

B y the time 1940 rolled around and we were on the verge of war, I had, by dint of strict application to correspondence courses and attendance at summer camps, reached the exalted rank of Captain of Cavalry, U.S. Army Reserve, and on July 26 of that year, I received orders to report to the commanding officer of the 1st Armored Division, Fort Knox, Kentucky, for assignment. There I was, in the army to stay for the next five years. I went overseas early in 1942, landing at Bone, Algeria, Africa,

Dick returned to military service in 1940, reaching the rank of Captain of Cavalry, U.S. Army Reserve.
Courtesy: Barbara Baker

*Dick on military
maneuvers in
Lousiana.*
Courtesy:
Barbara Baker

where I remained until the end of the African Campaign, which
wasn't long.

In the meantime, I had been promoted to Major, which led
directly to my being assigned as commanding officer of the 367th
Infantry Battalion with orders to take the battalion to Corsica.
Here, our duties were to protect the U.S. airfields. Since the situ-
ation was more or less stabilized on Corsica by then, I still don't
know from what danger we were protecting them.

Here, I had my first close contact with General de Gaulle. I had
seen "Le Grande Charles" a few times in Africa but when he came
to Corsica, I was appointed, along with certain others, as part of an
honorary staff to serve him. I took an instant dislike to the big tou-
can-nosed four-flusher, a feeling that I have never been relieved of.

We played a small part in the invasion of southern France and
then were transferred to Italy, where we remained until higher brass
decided to break up the 367th and distribute its various components
to other units. I was assigned to the State Department and sent to
Budapest, Hungary, as Military Advisor to the Minister of Hungary.

Some months prior to this assignment, I had been promoted to
Lieutenant Colonel. The end of the war found me still in Budapest,
where I remained until relieved in December 1945. I was sent to
Naples, Italy, to await transportation to the States. I came home
by boat, arriving at Norfolk, Virginia, late in December 1945.

Chapter 18

Home for Good

I got back to Snake River in early January 1946, and I haven't
been far from here since. This is my home, the only home I
ever had and the only one I ever wanted. My daughter, Barbara,
married Bob Terrill, and they have given me two fine grandsons,
so you might say we have taken root in this valley. I expect to fin-
ish up right here where there is no smog, no demonstrations and
a man can be friends with his children.

*Dick returned to his beloved Snake River, Wyoming, and took up
ranching and bronc riding.*

Courtesy: Barbara Baker

Courtesy:
Barbara Baker

Dick roping at Lander, Wyoming.

Courtesy: Barbara Baker

Dick sitting on a rock.
Courtesy: Barbara Baker

Dick was on the Moffat County Sheriff Posse for a few years.
Courtesy: Museum of Northwest Colorado

This photo of Dick's boots was taken in the living room at Mad Creek Ranch.

Courtesy: Barbara Baker

Chapter 19

Barbara's Turn

Written by Barbara Baker
Daughter of Richard and Virginia Barker

Richard Sutton Barker (Dick), who played the character Buster Brown, was born on December 6, 1899, in Framingham, Massachusetts, to Fletcher Barker and Beatrice Louise Sutton Barker. His mother worked for Brown Shoe Company, Inc., and traveled extensively selling shoes. Dick traveled with her. His father left the family shortly after Dick was born and, except for one time, Dick probably never saw him again. His mother never mentioned him to Dick. Beatrice Barker had been very well educated in Canada and the United States so she attempted to school Dick herself, so he never attended public schools. Dick said she would buy him any book or magazine that he wanted, and he early became an avid reader and probably gained much of his

---

Buster Brown shaking the hand of President Taft, which appears to be a cutout photo of the President.
Courtesy: Barbara Baker

education through books. At the age of seven, he began playing the Buster Brown character and traveled through every state in the union and to Alaska, singing and dancing and selling shoes, along with Tige.

At the age of 13, it was apparent he was too old to play the Buster Brown character anymore. He had a year of almost complete freedom as his mother went back on the road selling shoes and left him with her mother in St. Louis. They lived at the El Jovar Apartments across from the Botanical Gardens. Nana was quite old and Dick found it easy to escape to Lower Grove Park, where he fell in with a rather rough bunch of boys. They played football and baseball, pickup teams that played with more body contact than skill. The games usually ended in a free-for-all that, on a couple of occasions, took a squad of police to bring peace to the neighborhood. Nevertheless, it was good training for Dick, so that when he entered the eighth grade at Western Military Academy, he was ready for the coaching that would teach him the finer points of the game.

Dick had two summers of tutoring. Then in 1914, in order to catch up with his contemporaries, he enrolled at Dummer Academy, a school in South Byfield, Massachusetts. He finished his schooling there until the age of 15, when he enrolled in Western Military Academy in Alton, Illinois.

He apparently was an average student, making his way through the cadet ranks. He also played baseball. He lettered in this sport and was captain of the team his senior year. He played football and lettered in that also. At the age of 18, and in his final year at Western, he attended officer's training camp in Fort Sheridan, Illinois. After completing this course, he returned there as an instructor. He was too young to receive a commission, but he did receive an officer's pay.

After he was commissioned as a Lieutenant, he was appointed as an instructor at the University of Arkansas, Fayetteville, Arkansas. Dick graduated with his class at Western Military Academy in 1920. He received a nomination to West Point by Senator David I. Walsh, but much to the disappointment of his mother, he turned it down.

After graduating, he drifted around and tried to get back to Wyoming by catching a freight out of St. Louis. He got only as far as St. Joseph when the law picked him up for vagrancy. Since he was underage, they got in touch with his mother, who sent money to get him back to St. Louis. After three nights in the St. Joseph jail, according to Dick, it did not take much coaxing for him to produce his mother's address.

His first job was selling ribbons and other intimate items at Famous-Barr and Co., a large department store in St. Louis. That did not last more than an hour or so, and he left without the hour-and-a-half labor they owed him. Shortly after leaving the store, he met an old schoolmate from Western Military Academy, Bud Douglas. Bud lived in a small town about 30 miles east of St. Louis named Hillsboro. Hillsboro's main excuse for existence was the Eagle-Pitcher Zinc Smelter, a large company that hired a lot of men and supported a semipro baseball team. Dick went there and landed a job shoveling blue powder into the furnaces for three-and-a-half hours a day and played baseball for them the rest of the time. They did very well, winning 16 games and losing only one.

After getting what he thought was enough money to get him to Wyoming, he quit and took out for the West. He got as far as Oklahoma and went to work in the oil fields as a roughneck. Unfortunately, he got sick and had to return to St. Louis. He spent most of the next summer getting well and renewing old acquaintances from Western Military Academy.

One afternoon, a friend of his called and asked if he would like to go on a three-hour trip down the Mississippi on the riverboat, *St. Paul*. It was there that he met Vannie Virginia Spencer. Apparently it was love at first sight for both of them, and they were married on February 2, 1922. The day after they were married, the minister that married them was convicted of bootlegging.

Unfortunately, living for two was more expensive than living for one. Dick worked first at a filling station and then tried his hand as an auto mechanic. Neither job worked out. Dick had a friend named Haig Searcy, whose father was the head of the horse and mule department at the East St. Louis Stockyards. Haig got Dick a job there and, of course, it was more to his liking than anything previous. Virginia said that one time, he brought her a baby pig as a present. She loved it, but apparently their landlord did not. She also said that once a week, she would take a dollar and go to the store and buy two steaks, two potatoes and a loaf of bread as a special meal.

Dick's job was mostly cleaning stalls after the mules, an endless job, but he also got to ride horses all the time. This is where he first met Joker, one of his favorite horses. He also fell into another job that was not quite as legal. Across from the big main gate going into the stockyards and behind the local speakeasy there ran, day and night, a big craps game. So in addition to his other income, he got another $5.00 for working a short shift as a shill—that is, until the place was raided by the police and all were thrown in jail. The man that banked the game bailed them all out the next day, but Dick decided he had had enough of that fun, especially since he had to face Van (as he called Virginia) when he got home.

Dick finally decided it was time to go west, and he and Virginia left for Wyoming in 1923. He had become acquainted with a man named Herman Luyties. Herman had a homestead in Routt County near the Wyoming line. It was a couple of miles south of the Temple Ranch. Herman also had a small place near Morrison, outside of Denver, where he had a couple of horses. Dick and Herman agreed that Dick and Virginia would go to Denver, pick up the two horses and take them to Steamboat Springs by truck, and then ride them over to Snake River from there. They stayed one night with Millbank Frands at Clark, and then the next day rode over the hill above Three Forks and got a look at the valley that would be their home. They spent the first night at Luyties' cabin.

Unfortunately, Dick's partnership with Luyties did not work out and, as he often said, if it hadn't been for Mr. and Mrs. Harry Temple, they would probably have either starved to death or just given up and gone back to St. Louis. Mr. Temple gave Dick a job feeding cattle with his son, Pat, and Mrs. Temple took Virginia under her wing and taught her the finer points of ranch cooking, a talent that she continued to use for many years to come.

The following spring, Dick threw in with a bunch of men to run wild horses down in the Powder Wash area. The men were Wes Fleming, Shorty Creel, Guy McNurlin, Earnest Lang and Ed Niel. According to Dick, he was just along to learn. The object of collecting the horses was to make money but, as usual, things did not work out quite that way. They came up with a total of about

200 horses, drove them up the river to Baggs and corralled them in the Pendland corrals. Some of the horses belonged to upper country people and they were to get $5 a head for those but never did. They split up the rest and, of them, Dick got a team of bay mares named Polly and Peg and a little sorrel stud that he broke and his daughter rode to school for three years. He was called "Yellow Cat."

Dick decided that now was the time to get a place of his own, so he gave $1,500 for the old Fisher place of 220 acres and then homesteaded 640 acres to the south. The homestead was nothing but a log cabin with a dirt roof. Over the next few years, Dick—with occasional help from Virginia's brother, father and uncle—repaired the cabin into a fairly nice log home. (The relatives of Virginia all lived in Illinois and came out during the summer.) They built a barn, corrals and sheds. Dick's mother and Virginia's mother also visited occasionally. Dick's mother still had grandiose ideas, and since Virginia could play the piano, she bought her a grand piano. It almost took up the entire living room. In order to survive, Dick worked out [off the ranch[and Virginia gave piano lessons.

Dick simply could not make a living on the ranch, so he often went to work for the three dude ranches that were on the river—Boyers above Savery, Saddle Pocket Ranch that belonged to Ralph Salisbury and was above Slater, and later on the Focus Ranch that belonged to the Temples. They loved him! He charmed the dudes from the East with his stories and his humor. Many of the people that came out to the ranches kept in contact with him for years. This, of course, left Virginia at the age of 18 to 24 alone a lot of the time, until Barbara was born in 1929. She told many stories, too, of the winter when Dick was working away and she had nothing to eat but rutabagas from the garden. Another time she got hungry for some kind of meat, so she took the .22 out and shot the heads off of several doves and cooked them. Several times the gypsies came through. One time, they came in several horse drawn wagons and started to spread out over the buildings to see what they could steal. Virginia got Dick's .004, wrapped it in her apron and went out to meet them. She threatened them and the leader decided it would be better to leave, since she apparently had a pistol and it was pointed at him.

One of the ways that Dick and Virginia made ends meet was to play for dances on Snake River. Dick played the drums and Virginia played the piano. They played at the old Pep Hall that originally was close to Three Forks and was later moved down the river to above the Focus Ranch. They also played in Baggs and Dixon. Many of these dances were in the winter, so the trip was made in a horse-drawn sled. The dances at Pep Hall in the early 1920s were really the only recreation that the Snake River people had. They would bundle up their kids and make the

NEW YEAR'S DANCE

NEW YEAR'S EVE

BAGGS GYMNASIUM
Baggs, Wyoming

Music by **DICK BARKER**

Sponsored by . . .
Baggs I.O.O.F. Lodge
PRINTED IN CRAIG

Dick and Gin played for dances on Snake River for many years.
Courtesy: Barbara Baker

trip to the hall. Bunks had been built in the building so that the kids could go to bed while their parents danced. They usually had a supper at midnight and then danced until 2:00 a.m., or until Dick and Virginia played "Good Night Ladies."

Dick had a friend in these early years on Snake River. These are Dick's own words from his journal: "Years ago, I had a friend. According to present-day standards, he was worthless, crooked and altogether of no use to society, as we think of it. He was lusty, undependable and had the morals of a wild stud or an alley tom-cat, but he was also big, strong and entirely without fear of God or the devil. He could, would and did fight anyone either for him-self or his friends, without rancor and with a smiling joy that was a blessing to the majority who dreamed of being like him, but knew that the chemistry that went into their makeup made the very thought of being like him an utter impossibility. Anyway, he and I were going to steal a bunch of horses, drive them across the border into Mexico, sell them and get rich quick. After careful consideration of the consequences if we were caught, I chickened out. 'Hell' I said, 'what would Barbara and Virginia do if I went to prison, saying we got caught.' 'Oh, forget it,' said Norm, 'I wouldn't see Barbara's father go to prison. If we get caught, I'll take the rap.'" And knowing Norm Cochran, I'm sure he would have done just that.

During these years on upper Snake River, Dick had to go back in the army in order to keep up his commission in the Reserve Army and, of course, this also helped with the finances. The first time was in about 1935 when he went to Fort Bliss in El Paso, Texas. Virginia and Barbara went with him and stayed in a hotel while he was at camp. They drove down from the ranch on Snake River. As they drove along the highway in Texas, they came upon a turtle crossing the road. Dick said he thought he would stop and get it for Barbara. It would be a great pet. He got out of the car and started for it when the turtle raised itself up on its tiptoes and ran Dick right back into the car. Apparently, it was a snapping turtle and not very friendly.

During the 1930s, Dick had active duty in various places: Trinidad, Colorado; Fort Leavenworth, Kansas; Fort Bliss, Texas; Fort Carson, Colorado; and Montrose, Colorado, to name a few. Dick also had a tour of duty in a CCC (Civilian Conservation Corps) camp at Devil's Tower, Wyoming, around 1935, and then in 1937, another tour at a CCC camp in Meeker, Colorado. This was a bad year for him. Barbara came down with chickenpox and a few weeks later, Dick came down with it and then got pneumonia. He very nearly died and spent several weeks in the hospital in Grand Junction. He was just getting over that when he had a fall on a horse and broke his leg. This laid him up for about six weeks. Many years later, he started having trouble with his hip. After being x-rayed, it was discovered that he had at some early time broken his hip. Dick decided it was from that fall, but since he was on crutches due to his broken leg, the hip hadn't been noticed.

Dick had a tour of duty with the CCC (Civilian Conservation Corps) and was Commander at the camp in Meeker, Colorado.

Courtesy: Barbara Baker

In the winter of 1938, things were bad at the ranch, so Dick and Virginia decided to move to Arizona. Dick got a job on the Box O Ranch near Florence. When they first got to Arizona, they stopped at a huge adobe covered wagon that apparently had been a restaurant. The owners were looking for someone to open it up, so Virginia decided to do that while Dick worked on the Box O. The restaurant did not do well, so Virginia and Barbara moved into Florence, midway between Tucson and Phoenix, and also where the Arizona State Penitentiary is located. Barbara went to school there. After a year, they moved back to Snake River temporarily, and then in 1939, moved up Elk River near Steamboat Springs to the Mad Creek Ranch. Barbara went to school in Steamboat for a year.

By the time 1940 rolled around, Dick had accumulated enough time on active duty and various correspondence courses to be promoted to Captain. On July 26 of that year, he received orders to report to the 1st Armored Division at Fort Knox, Kentucky. The family headed east with a stop in Flora, Illinois, where Virginia and Barbara stayed for a short time with Virginia's mother and her brother, Lyle, and his wife. Barbara started school there, then they went on to Fort Knox to join Dick. Dick was sent on maneuvers to Lake Charles, Lousiana. Virginia and Barbara went along and Barbara went to school for a short time in Lake Charles.

Gin, Richard and Barbara at Fort Knox.

Courtesy: Barbara Baker

Dick was granted a leave after maneuvers and the family went to Boston to visit Dick's mother, who lived there with a family named Gott. On December 7, 1941, the Japanese attacked Pearl Harbor and President Roosevelt declared war on Japan. Dick immediately flew back to Fort Knox, leaving Virginia and Barbara in Boston. His seatmate on the flight down was Walter Winchell, a well-known radio news broadcaster. Dick did not realize who he was until they arrived in Louisville and the press immediately surrounded Winchell to ask him his views on the war.

Barbara went to school in Boston for a short time, and then she and Virginia drove down to Fort Knox. They purchased an 18-foot house trailer and settled down to life on another army post. Dick immediately began spending as much time as possible at the horse barns, riding and helping Barbara learn how to ride an English saddle and to learn jumping. Both Dick and Barbara entered several horse shows and won in various saddle and jumping classes.

Meanwhile, George Salisbury, Jr., who was a First Lieutenant in the army, and his wife, Laura, were ordered to Fort Knox. What a great day that was for Dick and Virginia, to have friends from Snake River close by! Laura was expecting a baby and soon had Georgie Salisbury III. Virginia and Laura became very close, a friendship that lasted until Virginia's death in 1986. One day, Dick and George managed to scrounge up some calves, and they spent the afternoon practicing roping in the riding arena, probably the first time that had ever been done on an army post.

Dick was always popular and well liked by the enlisted men, and this may be why he did not get along with his commander, General Henry. General Henry was regular army and regarded men under him as servants. Dick finally had enough and volunteered to go overseas in 1942. The family then made a last trip to Colorado taking their horses with them. Dick had bought a mare, Aroha, and her colt, Doughboy, from an army officer. As they drove out of Baggs, Wyoming, on their way back to Fort Knox, Dick stopped the car and got out and walked out through the sagebrush. He stopped and broke off a piece of the fragrant bush and put it in his wallet. He still had it when he returned from overseas. He said when he got homesick, he would get it out and the smell was still there.

The family resumed life in Fort Knox, waiting for Dick's orders to go overseas. Barbara was just getting over the measles when Dick called and said he was shipping out, and they could meet him briefly in Louisville at the train station. Virginia with Barbara, rash and all, met Dick and said goodbye as the train was leaving. They did not see him again for three years.

Dick landed in Bone, Algeria, Africa, where he remained until the end of the African Campaign. While there, as always, Dick managed to make lasting friends. This time it was with a French family named Barberousse. They had two daughters, Jeannine and Marie. Jeannine was the same age as Barbara and the two of them corresponded for a short time. The plan of the families was that Barbara would go to North Africa for a year of school and Jeannine would come to Colorado for a year. This, of course, was to be after the war. Shortly after Dick got back to Colorado at the end of the war, he received a printed letter bordered in black from the Barberousses saying that Jeannine had died of typhoid. The family was devastated, as was Dick.

Meanwhile, Dick had been promoted to Major and was assigned as commanding officer of the 367th Infantry Battalion. They were ordered to Corsica and played a small part in the invasion of southern France. When the 367th was broken up, Dick was assigned to the State Department and sent to Budapest, Hungary, as Military Advisor to the Minister of Hungary. By now, he had been promoted to Lieutenant Colonel.

The war was over and Dick was sent to Naples, Italy, and boarded the *SS Willia Floyd* that sailed for home on November 7, 1945. He arrived in Norfolk, Virginia, in late December 1945. He went to Denver and stayed with his friends, the Granbergs, for a few days and then went home to Steamboat Springs.

After Dick went overseas, Virginia and Barbara drove home to Colorado with their house trailer. They spent a year in Denver with the Granbergs and Barbara went to school at Smiley Jr. High. They went to Snake River for the summer and stayed at George and Emma Salisbury's ranch. Virginia helped with the cooking for the ranch hands and Barbara rode and helped with the ranch work. The next two summers, Virginia worked for Ralph and Marie Salisbury, cooking for their dudes. Meanwhile, Dick's mother, Beatrice

Barbara at their ranch in Wyoming.

Courtesy:
Barbara Baker

*Beatrice Barker
in her later years.*
Courtesy:
Barbara Baker

Barker, had moved to Steamboat and was living at a boardinghouse belonging to the Kitchens. The motel east of where she was living was for sale and Virginia bought it, and she and Beatrice ran it for the next couple of years. Barbara finished her high school in Steamboat.

After Dick came home in 1946, the first thing he wanted to do was get back to riding and ranching. He bought a small place, known as the McCollom place, west of Baggs, in the Powder Wash area. It had a barn and corrals and a part dugout for a threeroom cabin. Dick and Barbara spent the summer there riding while Virginia continued her work at the motel. Dick had become acquainted with Mr. Shefstead, father of Holmes and Guy. He had several horses that he wanted Dick to break to ride. Barbara and Dick gathered them up and drove them on the Great Divide Road to the ranch, with a stopover in Great Divide. They spent the next few months riding those horses and then returned them to the Shefsteads.

The summer of 1946 was a bad one for the Barkers. Barbara contracted polio and was taken to Colorado General Hospital in Denver for three months. When school started, Barbara took some classes that were offered at the hospital, as there were many children who had come down with this illness and were missing school. She returned to Steamboat in December and finished her senior year, graduating second in her class.

Unfortunately, it became apparent that the McCollom place would not support Dick and his family, so they sold it in 1950 to George Salisbury and moved to Gossard's Ranch south of Craig in Axial Basin. Dick worked for the Gossards, taking care of the ranch and cattle. Barbara spent most of the summer at George Salisbury's ranch on Snake River. It was at this time that she met Bob Terrill.

In the fall, Barbara went to Western State College and Bob went to Colorado State University. Dick and Virginia left the Gossard Ranch and moved to Rock River, Wyoming, on another ranch owned by the Salisburys. In the spring of 1948, Dick was called to active duty in Fort Knox. He and Virginia drove through Gunnison where Barbara was in school and, after some discussion about the joys of seeing the Kentucky Derby again, Barbara packed up and went with them.

Barbara contracted polio in the summer of 1946 and spent three months at Colorado General Hospital in Denver.
Courtesy: Barbara Baker

After that tour of duty, Dick and Virginia moved back to Snake River. Barbara taught school in Pleasant Valley near Steamboat for a year and Dick's mother lived with her.

Dick was again called to active duty, this time to Pittsburgh, Pennsylvania. They lived in an apartment and Dick commuted back and forth to work on the Pittsburgh public transportation. Every day, he rode with another man who was not in the army but was going to work in the general vicinity of where Dick worked. After riding with him for several weeks, the man asked Dick where he came from. Dick said a little town in Wyoming that he was sure would be unknown. The man said he might know it, was it near Baggs? Dick later said he almost fell over with surprise, but that was nothing compared to his next statement. The man said he had an uncle who lived in Baggs and his name was Martin Cull. Of course, Dick had known him for probably 40 years, and the stranger thing was that Martin was the last person from the river that Dick had talked to when he left for Pittsburgh.

After school was out in Pleasant Valley, Barbara took the train back to Pittsburgh. Dick's mother, who had traveled extensively by train most of her life, gave Barbara the finer points of Pullman travel. She insisted that Barbara have a suit, hat and white gloves for the trip. She explained about dining in the dining car and about the finger bowls that would be brought to the table after dinner. She said to be sure to tell the porter to wake her up in the morning, and not to be too surprised if a hand came through the curtain in her berth and gave the covers a shake. The porter would no doubt brush her hat with his little whisk and help her on and off the train. All was as her grandmother said.

Virginia and Barbara planned Barbara's spring wedding with Bob Terrill while in Pittsburgh. Of course, Dick had again found some friends, this time with people named Hopkins. They had two young sons. The two boys accompanied Dick and his family back to Colorado. They all stayed in Denver with Virginia's brother, Lyle, and his wife, Dorothy, until Barbara and Bob's wedding on June 28, 1949, at St. John's Cathedral Chapel. Barbara and Bob went on a short honeymoon to Cheyenne, Wyoming, and then moved to the McCollom place. Dick and Virginia had been living in Dixon in the house where Barbara had been born. They moved to Baggs and Dick ran the Texaco filling station for a while.

Dick learned of a position as a brand inspector in Idaho Falls, Idaho, and he and Virginia moved there for a short time. Neither he nor Virginia liked being so far from Colorado and Wyoming, so they moved to Lander in 1951, and Dick worked for the Yellowstone Sheep Co.

Virginia often went with Dick when he went out to feed the cattle with a sled and team. One cold morning, as they were putting the hay out, something frightened the team and they started running. Dick couldn't hold them, so he told Virginia to jump off in the snow. She did, but in doing so, she broke her leg. Dick managed to get the team stopped, but he had to leave her there in the middle of the feed ground with cattle all around while he went to the ranch to get the pickup so he could take her to the hospital. She said the cattle kept coming over and smelling her, trying to figure out what she was doing lying on their feed ground.

On April 28, 1951, Barbara and Bob had a baby boy named Patrick Hamilton Terrill. Barbara had wanted to name him Patrick Richard Terrill, but Bob refused. Barbara wanted to tell Dick of her desire, but she couldn't, because he would have known that Bob preferred his own dad's name. However, it also might have been that Bob had a hard time with the name Richard, because his older brother who had died tragically at the age of 13 was named Richard.

In November of 1952, Dick again applied for active duty so that he could continue to keep his Reserve status current. He was sent to San Diego and completed a course in Amphibious Warfare Indoctrination, for which he received a diploma.

In 1953, Dick got a job with Mountain Fuel Supply and went to work at the plant in Powder Wash. Even though it was not a job on a ranch, the pay was good and he had plenty of time with his horses. He built a small shed and corrals near the oil camp and spent his off hours there. He and "Gin" as Virginia was beginning to be called, were very well liked by the other employees. They had regular poker games and enjoyed the company of the people who lived and worked in Powder. Gin also started working at the cookhouse.

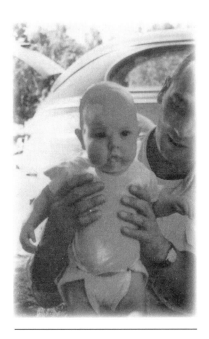

Bob and Pat Terrill in 1951.
Courtesy: Barbara Baker

Pat Terrill in 1962.
Courtesy: Barbara Baker

Pat Terrill in the 1980s.
Courtesy:
Barbara Baker

Barbara and Bob were now living in a mobile home in Powder Wash. They had lived for a year in the teacherage at Powder Wash, then moved back to the McCollom place, then again to the teacherage. The reason the teacherage was vacant was because Floy Hargrove was the teacher, and her husband Red, worked at Powder Wash and had a company house. When Floy and Red left Powder, the school needed the teacherage, so Bob and Barbara bought the mobile home and placed it in a space in the trailer park.

In 1954, Mountain Fuel transferred Dick to Hiawatha, where Gin had been given the cook house. Then in 1956 or '57 he was transferred to Sugar Loaf as a pumper. It was while he was here that he received the bad news from the army that he had 19 years, 4 months and 16 days of active duty and was therefore short the 20 years that he needed to retire. The army refused to give him his retirement pay. For the next 14 years, he wrote letters, recalculated his time and tried to get the army to recognize time that he knew he had.

On September 30, 1958, Dick and Virginia's second and last grandson, Timothy Mitchell, was born to Bob and Barbara Terrill. Bob and Barbara were still living in a mobile home in Powder Wash.

In 1960, much discouraged and tired of Mountain Fuel, Dick quit, and he and Virginia moved back to Dixon. They bought a little place there and Dick moved a barn in and built a corral. They opened the VFW bar. Dick, among

Tim Terrill in 1968.
Courtesy: Barbara Baker

other things, was mayor of Dixon for a time and then in 1971, he completed the Lower Court Training Conference and he was the local Justice of the Peace.

Some time back, he had become acquainted with Ham and Marge Regers. Ham was a retired Colonel in the army. He had placed an ad in the local paper asking for a U.S. Cavalry saddle, saddlebags and other regulation equipment. Dick happened to have the desired articles, so he called him. Ham seemed very much interested and said he would be in Craig soon. Of course, Ham bought the saddle and tack from Dick and while they were talking Ham found out about Dick not getting his retirement from the army. Ham went home and started a correspondence campaign with the army and finally, after several years of writing, the army decided Dick did have the time he had claimed and he received his retirement retroactive.

In 1963, Barbara and Bob had purchased a home in Craig and Pat was going to school there. Unfortunately, in 1958, Bob contracted diabetes and until his death in 1974, he was never very well.

Dick and Gin finally decided to move to Craig to be near Bob and Barbara, so Dick sold his property in Dixon and they rented a house in Craig for a short time and then purchased a mobile home. Dick still had his horses. At first, he kept them on some property in Dixon that Barbara owned, and when she sold it, he moved them to Stemp Springs, which is on the Medicine Bow Forest above Slater. This property was owned by Jim Cizak, a friend of Dick's, and he had purchased it from Henry Granberg, another longtime friend of Dick's. Dick went up several times a week to ride and take care of the horses.

Bob died in 1974. Dick and Gin remained close to Barbara and her two boys during these hard times.

In July of 1976, at the age of 76, Dick wrote in his journal that he was experiencing chest pains and felt he should go to the doctor, but he did not want to worry Gin. Then on July 24, 1976, he wrote, "I didn't go to the doctor after all because I've felt OK, and consequently don't want to make a big deal out of what probably is nothing worse than a good old-fashioned bellyache............ I am reminded of something I read years ago by an unknown writer who said:

My candle burns at both ends
It will not last the night,
But oh my friends and oh my foes
It makes a wonderful light."

Dick continued on, "a premonition of death? I have felt for some time that I'm getting to the end of my 'wonderful light.'"

On November 27, 1976, on the way back from Stemp Springs after spending, as Gin put it, "a wonderful day with the horses," Dick suffered a final heart attack and died on the way to Craig in the ambulance. His funeral was on December 1 (five days before he would have turned 77) and he is buried in Veteran's Cemetery in Craig. Gin, the love of his life, died after a long bout with cancer on March 4, 1984. She died on Barbara's birthday.

Dick Barker when he was leading the "Covered Wagon Tours" on the old trail at Fort La Clede, Wyoming, circa 1960.

Courtesy: Barbara Baker

Gin, in the center, went to Las Vegas after Dick's death. She is sitting with Sadie and Claude Ferguson.

Courtesy: Barbara Baker

Barbara Terrill served as Moffat County's Clerk and Recorder from 1970 to 1990.
Courtesy: Barbara Baker

Barbara married Bob Baker in 1984.

Courtesy: Barbara Baker

Hartke & Sheets Saddle—
circa 1890

When Richard Barker was in his later years, he suffered a broken hip that gave him some trouble. In the early 1960s after hip surgery, he found that this old saddle, which he had discovered in the basement of the Bank Club Bar in Baggs, was the only one that could give him a comfortable ride.

This saddle is one of the few examples known to be in existence from these two Meeker saddle makers. This A-fork loop seat, high-cantle saddle is an excellent illustration of the work of these two men. It is left to the imagination to wonder what type of "life" this 100-year-old saddle led and what ranges it saw before its use by Dick Barker and its subsequent "retirement" to a quiet museum display.

*This Hartke &
Sheets saddle,
circa 1890,
was ridden
by Dick
Barker in his
later years. It
is one of only
a few existing
saddles made
by these
Meeker saddle
makers. It is
on display at
the Museum
of Northwest
Colorado.*
Courtesy:
Museum of
Northwest
Colorado

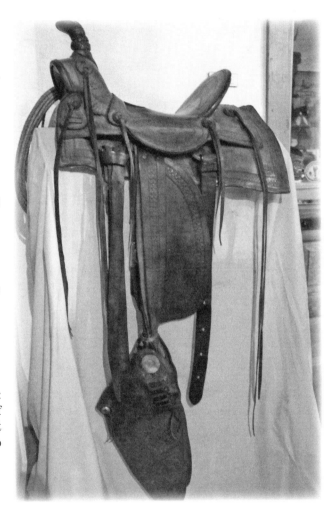

Buster Brown
and the
Cowboy

Timeline

1899   Richard Barker born December 6 in Massachusetts

1907   Richard hired as Buster Brown at age 7

1913   At age 14, Richard's last appearance as Buster Brown in Yuma, Arizona

1915   Richard enters Western Military Academy

1917   Richard enlists in U.S. Army for World War I

1920   Discharged after the war, Richard returns to the Academy to graduate

1923   Comes into the Snake River Valley with his sixteen-year-old bride, Virginia

1940   Returns to active service in the army for 5 years

1976   Richard Barker dies at the age of 76